For Lotje and Julia, who make my life spatter – JG

JESSE GOOSSENS & LINDE FAAS

Cola Fountains and Spattering Paint Bombs

47 EXPERIMENTS   TO DO AT HOME

LEMNISCAAT 8 USA

All experiments in this book have been
described and/or carried out on the Internet
by various people.
Great sites with a lot of experiments include:
www.growingajeweledrose.com
www.hunkinsexperiments.com
www.sciencebob.com
www.sciencekids.co.nz
www.stevespanglerscience.com
www.thenakedscientists.com
www.livescience.com
www.chemistry.about.com

First published in the United States in 2016

Text © 2015 Jesse Goossens
Illustrations © 2015 Linde Faas
This edition copyright © 2016 Lemniscaat
USA
Dutch rights Lemniscaat b.v., Vijverlaan 48,
3062 HL Rotterdam
ISBN 978 90 477 0721 9
Lithography: Pixel-It, Zutphen
Printing and binding: Wilco, Amersfoort

Goossens, Jesse
Cola Fountains and Spattering Paint Bombs / Jesse
Goossens ; illustrated by Linda Faas ;
translated by Jonathan Ellis
p. 108 ; color ; illustrations ; cm.
1. Science – Experiments – Juvenile literature.
2. Scientific recreations – Juvenile literature.

Q164   507.8
ISBN 978-1-935954-52-1

Designed by Marc Suvaal
Manufactured by Worzalla Printing, Stevenspoint, WI
Printed in the United States of America

Distributed in the U.S. by Ingram Publisher Services
14 Ingram Blvd, La Vergne, TN 37086

WWW.LEMNISCAATUSA.COM

CONTENTS

THE MEASUREMENTS

To make things easy, this book uses cups and spoons.
If you want to be really exact:

1 cup = 225 ml
1 tablespoon = 15 ml
1 teaspoon = 5 ml

THE SYMBOLS

Note the symbols next to each experiment

explodes

requires heat or fire

takes a long time (longer than an hour)

messy

do this outside

put on your safety goggles

super easy

easy

difficult

All of the experiments in this book require adult supervision, and some require careful, hands-on adult assistance. Even materials that might not appear dangerous can be harmful in certain situations if mixed, or if used improperly. Any experiments using fire are safest performed outside and require particular adult assistance and attention. Some materials and experiments may endanger people or pets, either in the process of doing them or if left unattended or stored improperly. Get adult help to decide which ones are right for you, and make sure an adult is there helping along the way. Read through the experiment completely before starting.

COLA FOUNTAIN
THE COLA WILL SHOOT OUT OF THE BOTTLE!

WHAT YOU NEED:
a bottle of diet cola | a roll of Mentos | a sheet of paper

WHAT DO YOU DO?

Open the bottle of cola and put it outside, either on the ground or on a table. Make sure it can't fall over.

Undo all of the Mentos in the roll.

Roll them up in a piece of paper like a tube. Make the roll the same width as the mouth of the bottle.

Stand the paper on top of the open bottle so that the Mentos drop in all at once. Run away!

WHY DOES IT WORK?

Cola contains carbon dioxide. That's what causes the little bubbles that tickle your tongue when you drink it.

Carbon dioxide looks for somewhere to attach itself in order to make bubbles. The bottle is smooth, but each Mentos candy has some forty layers of sugar which form a rough surface. That's where the carbon dioxide attaches and creates a whole lot of bubbles— all of them want to escape from the bottle at once!

Because the Mentos sink to the bottom, the bubbles are formed under the cola. Those bubbles expel the cola with an enormous whoosh from the bottle.

9

DANCING RAISINS

DID YOU KNOW THAT RAISINS CAN BOOGIE?

WHAT DO YOU DO?

Place the jar on a plate to catch any spills.

Fill the jar two thirds full of water.

Add 3 teaspoons of baking soda, stir until it dissolves.

Add 8-10 raisins.

Stir in 5 tablespoons of vinegar.

After a few minutes, the raisins will start dancing! (If nothing happens, try adding a little more baking soda or vinegar.)

Instead of raisins, you can try pieces of broken spaghetti.

WHY DOES IT WORK?

Raisins would sink to the bottom in a jar filled with water. By adding vinegar and baking soda (bicarbonate) together, carbon dioxide gas is created that rises to the surface as bubbles. Those bubbles make the raisins dance.

WHAT YOU NEED: ⚗

baking soda | vinegar | small box of raisins | water
a glass jar (a quart) | a teaspoon | a tablespoon

PAINT BOMBS
TURN YOUR DOORSTEP INTO A PAINTING!

> **WHAT YOU NEED:**
> corn starch | hot water | vinegar | food coloring or tempera paint
> baking soda | sandwich-size plastic bags such as Ziploc
> a tablespoon | a cup | paper towels

WHAT DO YOU DO?

Put 1 tablespoon of baking soda on a paper towel and fold the towel into an envelope.

Pour ½ cup vinegar into a plastic bag and add food coloring or tempera paint.

Mix in ¾ cup corn starch until you have a gooey mess.

Add ¼ cup hot water.

Close the bag, leaving a small opening.

Push in the paper towel envelope with the baking soda and seal the bag.

Place the bag on the ground. Stand back and watch as it blows up.

Didn't it work? Shaking the bag can work wonders, but you might get covered in paint.

WHY DOES IT WORK?

The acid from the vinegar and the bicarbonate in the baking soda form carbon dioxide, a gas. This produces so much gas that it doesn't all fit into the bag. That's why the bag grows and grows until it explodes.

ZOOOOOOOOOOOMMMM!

WHY DOES IT WORK?

The air in the balloon escapes through the bottle nozzle and the hole in the CD. As air is pushed between the floor and the CD. It starts to move just like a hovercraft.

THIS SILVER HOVERCRAFT WILL BE FLYING IN MINUTES!

FLYING SAUCER

WHAT DO YOU DO?

Have an adult stick the nozzle to the CD with the super glue—never touch super glue yourself because it can be dangerous. Ask the adult to make sure the hole in the nozzle is centered above the hole in the CD.

When the glue is dry, place the CD on a smooth floor (tile or wood, not carpet).

Blow up the balloon and slip the mouthpiece over the bottle nozzle or blow up the balloon through the hole in the CD.

Let go and watch the CD fly over the ground like a hovercraft.

WHAT YOU NEED: 🧪🧪🧪

a CD | the plastic nozzle from a water bottle
super glue | a balloon

SPEWING VOLCANO

MAKE A VOLCANO ERUPT!

SPEEEEEWWW!

WHAT YOU NEED:

For the volcano: glue | paint | a plastic soda bottle | newspapers
For the lava: baking soda | vinegar | orange food coloring or tempera paint | a jug | a cup | a tablespoon | a funnel

WHAT DO YOU DO?

You can use a plain bottle for this experiment, but it's a lot more fun if you turn it into a real volcano. Glue newspapers to the bottle to form a mountain, making sure to leave the mouth of the bottle uncovered. Paint it to look like your very own volcano.

In a jug, mix together 1 cup of vinegar and some orange paint or food coloring.

Insert the funnel into the opening of the volcano and add 4 tablespoons of baking soda.

Then, pour in the orange vinegar as quickly as possible and remove the funnel.

WHY DOES IT WORK?

The vinegar and baking soda combine to form carbon dioxide, which makes everything fizz and foam. As more foam is created, it's pushed out of the bottle to stream down the volcano as lava.

*NOT FOR HUMANS!

ELEPHANT TOOTHPASTE*

HAVE YOU EVER WONDERED WHAT ELEPHANTS USE TO CLEAN THEIR TEETH? NOT THIS, BUT IT'S STILL FUN TO MAKE!

WHAT DO YOU DO?

Put the bottle in a place where you can make a mess (outside or in large tub).

Ask an adult to pour ½ cup of hydrogen peroxide into the bottle.

Add some food coloring or tempera paint, and squirt in a little bit of dish soap.

In a small bowl, mix one teaspoon (or packet) of dry yeast with two teaspoons of warm water.

Pour the yeast mixture into the bottle and bring on the elephants!

WHY DOES IT WORK?

Hydrogen peroxide changes into water and oxygen. Yeast makes that happen even faster. Oxygen changes the dish soap into foam.

If you feel the bottle, you'll notice that it's getting warm. During this process, energy is released in the form of heat.

19

NAKED EGG

YOU CAN EVEN GET THIS RAW EGG TO BOUNCE!

WHAT YOU NEED: 🕐 ⚗️
an egg | vinegar | a glass

BOINGBOINGBOIN

20

WHAT DO YOU DO?

Put the egg in the glass. Pour in enough vinegar to cover the whole egg. The egg might start to float a little.

You'll see tiny bubbles forming on the eggshell. After a while, a white foam-like layer will appear on the vinegar.

After 24 hours, carefully remove the egg from the vinegar. The easiest way to do that is to hold your hand above a sink and pour everything onto it. You can brush off anything sticking to the egg with your finger. If you put your egg into a fresh layer of vinegar and allow it to soak for an extra day, it will be even stronger.

You now have a naked egg–the outside is rubbery, and if you hold it above the table and drop it gently, you will see that it actually bounces!

Be careful: the egg is still raw, so it can break. Be sure to thoroughly wash your hands when you are done.

WHY DOES IT WORK?

The shell of an egg is mostly calcium carbonate, a salt that dissolves in acid. The acidic vinegar makes the eggshell dissolve, leaving the thin skin around the egg, the membrane, which holds the egg together. You also see the membrane when you boil and egg and remove the shell.

The egg has become a little bigger because vinegar has seeped through the membrane into the egg.

GROWING CRYSTALS

IT TAKES A WHILE, BUT THE CRYSTALS ARE WORTH THE WAIT!

WHAT YOU NEED: 🕐 ⚗⚗⚗

eggshells, broken in half, washed, and dried | an egg carton | glue | powdered alum | water | food coloring (optional) | a kettle | a brush | a small bowl | a cup

WHAT DO YOU DO?

Using a brush, cover the inside of the eggshells with glue.

Sprinkle the wet glue with a thick layer of powdered alum.

Place the shells in the egg carton and leave them to dry overnight.

Get an adult to dissolve ¾ cup of powdered alum in two cups of boiling water in a bowl.

When the solution has cooled, add a squirt of food coloring and put the eggshells into the water so that they are submerged. Leave them to soak overnight.

The next day, remove the eggshells from the alum solution. The first crystals have grown!

If you want your crystals to grow bigger, put them in the alum solution for another night. You can do this as often as you like.

In this way, you can make crystals with a variety of colors, shapes, and sizes by brushing different objects with glue and following the same procedure.

WHY DOES IT WORK?

Powdered alum is made up of tiny crystals. When these tiny crystals are dissolved in warm water, they separate into teeny tiny pieces (molecules). When the water starts to evaporate, the molecules get together, and form larger crystals. They attach themselves to the alum that was glued onto the eggshells–the longer you wait, the more water evaporates, and the bigger the crystals grow.

COLA BALLOON

WILL THE COLA BURST YOUR BALLOON?

WHAT DO YOU DO?

Pour a few teaspoons of salt through the opening of an empty balloon, making sure not to spill any.

Open the cola and slip the balloon as far as you can over the bottle.

Hold the balloon upright so the salt falls into the cola.

Then watch what happens!

Can your balloon take it?

Try it with sugar instead of salt. Do you notice a difference?

WHAT YOU NEED:
one bottle of cola (diet works best) or other soda
a balloon | salt | a teaspoon

WHY DOES IT WORK?

Cola contains carbon dioxide. It's what makes the hissing noise when you open the bottle.

If you pour salt (or sugar) into soda, the carbon dioxide attaches itself to the grains and produces a lot of gas. This makes the soda bubble and blow up the balloon.

If your balloon doesn't burst, you'll see the soda gradually calm down. The soda has gone flat so the soda runs back into the bottle.

SHHHH!

GLITTER SLIME

MAKE SOME OOEY, GOOEY GLITTERY SLIME!

WHAT YOU NEED:
glitter glue | borax crystals | water | a teaspoon
a tablespoon | a cup | a bowl | a glass jar with a lid,
or a plastic bag

GLITTERG

WHAT DO YOU DO?

Borax crystals are slightly poisonous so make sure you stay out of the way of any food.

With the help of an adult, mix 1 teaspoon of borax crystals in 1 cup of water.

Squeeze a tube (about 225 ml) of glitter glue (or a mixture of school glue and glitter) into a bowl. Mix in 1 tablespoon of water.

Pour the borax mixture into the glue and knead it.

When your glitter slime feels ready, take it out of the water.

If it's too slimy, put it back into the water and it will get harder.

If you want to save your slime, store it in a container with a lid, or in a plastic bag that you can tie closed, and keep it out of reach of other children and pets. Wash your hands thoroughly after this one!

WHY DOES IT WORK?

Glitter glue contains tiny bits of plastic (fancy name: polyvinyl acetate). Borax is a mineral salt that joins the small plastic particles together forms a squishy plastic mass.

BATHTUB BUBBLY BALL

TAKING A BATH IS EVEN MORE FUN WITH SELF—MADE BUBBLY BALLS!

WHAT YOU NEED: ⏲ 🥽 ⚗⚗⚗

corn starch | baking soda | mineral salt | citric acid
scented oil (optional) | food coloring (optional)
whisk (optional) | a cup | a bowl | a spray bottle filled with
water | a silicone baking tray with fun shapes

BUBBLEBUBBLEFIZZZ

WHAT DO YOU DO?

In a bowl, mix together ½ cup corn starch, 1 cup baking soda, ½ cup salt and ½ cup citric acid. Make sure there are no lumps in the mixture–a whisk can really help. Be careful not to get any citric acid in your eyes, because it really stings!

Dribble some (optional) scented oil and food coloring into the powder mixture.

Spray some water to the mixture so that it is just wet enough so that everything sticks together. Add a little at a time to get the best results. If you use too much water, the balls will be less bubbly in the bath.

Spoon and press the mixture into the baking tray.

Leave it to harden for a few hours. Take the bubble balls out of the tray and you're ready to take a bath!

WHY DOES IT WORK?

As you sprayed water into the mixture, you might have noticed it start to bubble just a bit. When a mixture of citric acid and baking soda comes into contact with water, carbon dioxide is formed, the same gas that makes soda bubble.

If you throw a ball containing citric acid and baking soda into your bath, carbon dioxide is formed, and this makes the bathwater bubble like soda.

ZZZZZ!

STORM IN A JAR
WATCH IT WHIRL EVERY TIME YOU SHAKE IT!

WHAT YOU NEED:
water | dish soap | a glass jar with a lid

WHAT DO YOU DO?

Fill a glass jar three quarters with water.

Add a squeeze of dish soap to the water and screw the lid onto the jar.

Give the jar a good shake, until the water is foamy.

Watch carefully—you've made your very own whirlpool.

Every time you shake the jar, the whirlpool will appear!

WHY DOES IT WORK?

When you shake the jar, the water starts revolving. The force with which the water spins pushes the water against the sides of the jar. That's known as centrifugal force.

Because the water in the jar is pressed against the sides of the jar, there is a space in the middle into which the foam streams, causing a vortex. A tornado is also a vortex, but is caused by streams of air instead of water and foam.

MATCH ROCKET

SHOOT A MINI-ROCKET A LONG WAY!

WHAT DO YOU DO?

Cut a strip of aluminum foil that is about the same length as a match and about the width of half a match-length.

Have an adult help you place the match across the width of the aluminum foil making sure the head is exactly in the middle of the foil.

Place a needle against the match, with the point about halfway along the match head.

Now roll the top part of the match, together with the needle, in the foil.

Give the foil above the head of the match an extra twist.

Press the foil against the needle and then pull out the needle, so that a very tiny air passage is left in the foil. Make sure you don't press it together!

Bend the paper clip so that you can lean the match lean against it, like a launching pad.

Have an adult hold a burning match under the aluminum foil containing the head of the rocket. Stand back!

And...

(It may not work the first time, but keep trying!)

Be careful when you pick it up after it lands—the rocket gets red hot!

10-9-8-7-6-5-4-3-2-1-1-LIFTOFF!

WHY DOES IT WORK?

The heat causes the head of the match to ignite inside the foil. Because the fire is in the aluminum foil, the smoke and gas that is released has nowhere to go. This causes enormous pressure inside the aluminum rocket. That pressure finds an exit through the small passageway left by the needle, and this launches the match.

33

COLA CONCOCTION

LET'S SEE IF YOU STILL LIKE COLA AFTER THIS!

WHAT DO YOU DO?

Unscrew the cap on the cola bottle.

Pour milk into the cola bottle right up to the top and screw the cap back on.

Leave the bottle for a few hours—the longer, the better.

Be honest, would you want to drink it?

WHY DOES IT WORK?

Cola contains phosphorous, a substance that can be used to remove rust. That's why rust disappears from metal if you leave it in cola for awhile.

The milk attaches itself to the phosphorous. This makes the milk curdle and then it sinks to the bottom of the cola. What's left of the milk and cola forms the yellowy transparent top layer.

SSS!

WHAT YOU NEED:
a small bottle of cola | milk

35

BOUNCY BALL

POWDERS AND LIQUIDS TURN INTO A BOUNCY BALL!

BOING!

WHAT DO YOU DO?

Have an adult mix two tablespoons of hot water with ½ teaspoon of borax crystals in a bowl. Be careful—borax crystals are poisonous, so don't put your fingers into your mouth or touch food until you've washed your hands thoroughly.

Stir until the borax crystals are dissolved as much as possible. Add a squirt of food coloring if you like.

Put one tablespoon of glue into a bowl. Add—without mixing!—½ teaspoon of the borax-water mixture and 1 tablespoon of corn starch.

Allow the mixture to stand for 15 seconds.

Then start stirring, until it becomes a lumpy mess. Use your hands to knead it, as quickly as you can, into a ball.

You will notice it becomes stiff very quickly.

Now bounce away!

Keep your bouncy ball in a closed plastic bag when you're finished playing with it, and out of reach of other children and pets.

WHY DOES IT WORK?

Corn starch contains a type of sugar–amylopectin—a starch that works like an elastic binding agent. The school glue contains polyvinyl acetate, a pliable plastic that is also found in chewing gum. The borax crystals connect this pliable plastic with the elastic binding agent (amylopectin). This turns it into a rubbery mass that can bounce.

FLOATING MS

REMOVE THE Ms FROM YOUR M&Ms!

WHAT YOU NEED:
M&M candies | water | a shallow dish or soup plate

M   M   M

WHAT DO YOU DO?

Pour a layer of water into a dish.

Place a couple of M&Ms into it (for example, four different colors).

Make sure the M&Ms are not too close together.

Wait and watch what happens.

Which color is the first to release the M?

WHY DOES IT WORK?

A colored sugar coating covers each M&M. The letter M is then printed on it with an edible ink.

The sugar layer dissolves in the water. You can see that from the color that floats from each M&M.

Because the sugar layer dissolves, the ink M separates and floats to the surface.

M M M !

WATER SAND

MAKE UNDERWATER ART!

WHAT YOU NEED:

fine sand (colored sand works best) | a spray can of fabric protector (such as Scotch Guard) | parchment paper (for baking)
water | a glass bowl | a jar with a lid

WHAT DO YOU DO?

Do this outside or with the door wide open for ventilation.

Place a pile of sand on a piece of parchment paper. If you have sand in different colors, tear off several smaller pieces of baking paper to make separate piles.

Spray the fabric protector onto the sand—be careful not to breathe the fumes. Mix the sand and spray again until all the sand is wet.

Leave the sand to dry for an hour.

Your water sand is ready! If you pour it into a glass bowl filled with water, you'll get a surprise.

Water sand remains dry in the water!

When you're done playing, you can take the sand out and put it on a piece of newspaper to dry. Store it in the jar and you can play with it again and again.

WHY DOES IT WORK?

Fabric protector is a liquid that applies a thin layer that repels dirt and water. By spraying grains of sand on all sides with fabric protector, you give them water repellent layers. If you throw this water-repellent sand into water, it remains dry and the water can't attach itself to it.

EXPLODING EGG
LOOK OUT! IT'S AN EGG—SPLOSION!

WHAT DO YOU DO?

Place the egg in the glass and pour in enough vinegar to cover it completely.

Leave it for one or two days—the longer, the better. It works best if you pour in fresh vinegar each day.

Remove the egg from the vinegar and wash it under a gentle stream of water to get rid of the last pieces of eggshell.

Put the egg in an egg-cup and prick it with a skewer.

If you want to make an even bigger effect, soak it an additional day in karo syrup and water. The egg will be smaller. Then soak it in water and watch it expand even more. Then prick it and see what happens!

When the egg has finished spraying, you can squeeze it to make it spray some more. Make sure to clean up thoroughly, and wash your hands well when you're done!

WHY DOES IT WORK?

We explained in the "Naked egg" experiment on page 20 why the eggshell dissolves in vinegar. The egg has become a little bit bigger because vinegar has seeped through the membrane into the egg. The membrane—the skin that keeps the egg together—is now under considerable pressure and if you prick it with a skewer, the contents shoot out.

SPRROOOSSSSSH!

MILK PLASTIC

MAKE PLASTIC IN YOUR KITCHEN!

WHAT YOU NEED:

milk | vinegar | food coloring, glitter, beads etc. (optional)
a saucepan | a tablespoon | a cup | a sieve | cookie cutters
(optional) | a wooden spoon | aluminum foil or wax paper

PLASTICFANTAST

WHAT DO YOU DO?

Pour 1 cup of milk into a saucepan. If you like, add some food coloring.

Get an adult to heat up the milk for you but don't let it boil.

Stir in 1 tablespoon of vinegar.

You'll see that the milk will curdle and form a thick, white, transparent mess.

Have the adult pour the mixture into a sieve over the sink.

Then use the back of your spoon to press out the last drops of liquid from the white ooze.

You've now got a sort of grainy clay. Use it to make whatever you like—a keychain or jewelry or whatever appeals to you. You could even roll it flat and cut shapes from it. You can also decorate it with glitter or push beds into it.

The thinner the shapes, the quicker they dry and the better they turn out.

Leave them to dry for two days on wax paper or aluminum foil.

WHY DOES IT WORK?

Milk contains casein protein. The acid in the vinegar causes the proteins to form clots (coagulate) and turn into a white ooze. When you put the mixture through a sieve, you are left with the casein goo, which turns hard if you leave it long enough.

In the first half of the twentieth century, milk plastic (casein plastic) was used to make a whole lot of things from pens to jewellery.

TASTY CRYSTAL LOLLIPOPS

THESE SWEETS ARE PRETTY and TASTY!

LOLLY

L

WHAT YOU NEED:
Demerara sugar (raw sugar) | water | a saucepan | a cup | a jar
a popsicle stick (or some other stick) | tape | a wooden spoon

46

WHAT DO YOU DO?

Ask an adult to put a saucepan on the cooker. Pour in 1 cup of water and 3 cups of Demerara sugar.

Have the adult stir until the sugar has dissolved.

The adult should take the saucepan from the burner and pour the liquid into the jar. Caution—this is very hot!

Stick a piece of tape over the middle of the opening of the jar.

Attach the Popsicle stick to the middle of the tape and let the other end hang in the liquid (use as much tape as you need). Make sure the stick doesn't touch the bottom or the sides of the jar.

Put the jar in a place where it can stand for a couple of days.

Check on your lollipop each day to see how much it has grown.

When you really can't wait any longer, take a lick!

WHY DOES IT WORK?

The sugar is dissolved in the water. When water stands around for a while, it starts to evaporate, but sugar doesn't evaporate. If there is too little water for all the sugar to dissolve in, some of the sugar attaches itself to the rough surface of the stick.

As more and more water evaporates, the sugar crystals on the stick get bigger and bigger.

CKYLIKEY!

LAVA LAMP

THIS WAS SUPER HIP IN THE 60s!

> **WHAT YOU NEED:**
> vegetable oil | water | an Alka-Seltzer or other effervescent tablet
> food coloring | a clear jar or bottle

WHAT DO YOU DO?

Fill the jar or bottle a quarter of the way with water.

Add the oil until the jar or bottle is almost full. You'll notice that the oil will float on the water.

Add a few drops of food coloring to the oil.

Break an effervescent tablet into pieces and throw them into the liquid one at a time.

Watch the lava's groovy moves!

Tip: Don't shake the jar, because then you will break the bubbles.

BLUB — B

WHY DOES IT WORK?

Oil and water don't mix because they each have a different density. Water has a lot more molecules than the same amount of oil—it's heavier so the oil starts to float on it.

When you throw pieces of the effervescent tablet into the water, it forms a gas with the water.

The water-gas bubbles are lighter than the oil and break through the oil layer to get to the surface. The gas escapes and the water sinks back down to the bottom.

As long as the tablets continue to fizz, the lava lamp will keep moving.

UB — BLUB!

TEA BAG ROCKET
THE EASIEST ROCKET!

WHAT DO YOU DO?

Cut off the top of the tea bag. Make sure that the bottom of the tea bag isn't stuck together.

Shake the tea into a cup (somebody can use it later).

The paper of the bag now forms a round tube. Stand it up on the ground.

Have an adult light the top with a match, stand back, and wait.

If the tea bag falls over, then it won't work, but if it remains upright:

WHY DOES IT WORK?

When the tube is lit, the air in the tube is heated. Hot air rises. Once it has started to burn and become lighter, the hot air makes it blow upwards.

FLAMINGFIREFLY!

WHAT YOU NEED:
a flow-through tea bag like Lipton's | matches
a pair of scissors | a cup

DANCING OOBLECK

THIS BLUBBER DANCES TO THE VIBRATION OF TONES!

WHAT YOU NEED:

corn starch | water | food coloring (optional) | a cup | a dish | a thin metal tray or baking sheet | an audio player (such as MP3) with a speaker

OOOOOOOO

52

WHAT DO YOU DO?

First make the oobleck. This is a strange mixture celebrated in a book by Dr. Seuss, *Bartholomew and the Oobleck*. In a bowl, mix 2 cups of corn starch with 1 cup of water.

Now download a number of test tones to your audio player. Try a site like www.audiocheck.net.

Place a tray or baking sheet on your speaker. Pour in the oobleck.

Play a test tone. What happens?

What happens if you play a different tone?

Try dribbling some food coloring onto mixture.

Turn on the test tones again and let the oobleck dance!

You can also see which music the oobleck responds to most, but test tones work best.

WHY DOES IT WORK?

Sound causes vibrations. The oobleck is thin enough to be set in motion by the vibrations, yet thick enough to remain one mass. You can actually see the sound vibrations come to life.

Because every tone causes a different vibration, the oobleck dances better to certain tones.

BLECH!

54

FOAM SNAKES

YOU'VE NEVER BLOWN BUBBLES LIKE THIS!

WHAT DO YOU DO?

Cut the bottle in half. Throw away the bottom half.

Stretch the sock over the bottom of the top half of the bottle and tape it firmly.

In a dish, mix ½ cup of dish soap with 2 cups of water and 2 teaspoons of sugar.

Dip the sock in the mixture and let it drain for a few seconds.

Blow through the neck of the bottle.

After dipping the sock, you can squirt some food coloring onto it to give your snake a special shade!

WHY DOES IT WORK?

The sugar makes the bubbles tougher, so they last longer.

FOAM BUBBLY COOL!

POTTED VOLCANO
A MINIATURE ERUPTION!

> **WHAT YOU NEED:**
> a candle (can also be colored) | matches | sand
> water a fireproof glass jar or beaker | a hotplate or stovetop burner

WHAT DO YOU DO?

Light the candle and let the candle wax drip into the middle of the glass jar.

When you have created a nice layer of candle wax, cover it with a layer of sand.

Fill the jar with water.

Have an adult put the jar on the hotplate or burner.

Watch the volcano form in the jar and eventually erupt.

WHY DOES IT WORK?

The heat makes the candle wax melt. The liquid candle wax works itself upwards through the sand, which causes a small eruption. The cold water causes the candle wax to turn hard again.

CLAY QUICKSAND

ONE MINUTE IT'S CLAY AND THE NEXT IT'S LIQUID!

WHAT DO YOU DO?

In a bowl, mix 1 cup of sand with 1 cup of corn starch.

Add a little bit of paint to it–not too much–and knead it until it forms a ball that sticks together.

You can add a tiny bit of water if needed, not too much.

Your clay quicksand is ready. Think of it as a sandy oobleck!

You can mold it and shape it as you knead, but if you leave it alone, it turns into mud.

SLIPPYSLIP

WHY DOES IT WORK?

Corn starch contains a starch that works like an elastic binding agent. The corn starch binds the paint (and the water, if you've added it) with the sand as you knead and mold.

When you stop kneading it, the liquid, the sand, and the corn starch separate, and it all becomes liquid. Once you start kneading it again, it turns back into clay.

WHAT YOU NEED:

fine sand (play sand) | corn starch | water
washable liquid paint | a cup | a bowl

SLURPY SAND!

59

SWIRLY STORM

WHAT DO YOU DO?

Get an adult to heat up a kettle or bowl of water until it starts to steam.

Have the adult pour the hot water into the jar, until it's about one third full.

Place the lid upside down on the jar and put the ice cubes on the lid.

Have an adult squirt a little of the spray into the jar, and then quickly put the lid back on.

There's your cloud—

WHY DOES IT WORK?

The heat causes the water to evaporate. Hot air rises. In the jar, the hot air comes up against the ice-cold lid and starts to fall again. If the air is to turn back into water, it needs something to attach itself to. The water forms around the particles that came from the spray can and sinks to the bottom of the jar.

CLOUD IN A JAR

WATCH CLOUDS FORM RIGHT BEFORE YOUR EYES!

WEATHER!

WHAT YOU NEED:

water | ice cubes | a spray can (for example, air freshener or deodorant) | a small saucepan or bowl a stovetop or microwave | a glass jar with a lid

GREEN MONEY

TURN PENNIES GREEN!

WHAT DO YOU DO?

Cover the bottom of the plate with a paper towel. Place a few pennies on it.

Pour vinegar over the coins until the paper towel is completely saturated.

Leave it overnight.

Every day the pennies will become greener. Turn them over occasionally, adding more vinegar so that when the paper dries, they will be even greener. Be careful not to touch your eyes, nose, or mouth after handling the coins, and make sure to wash your hands well afterwards or use tweezers or rubber gloves.

WHAT YOU NEED: pennies | vinegar | a deep plate | paper towels

GREEDY GREEN

62

WHY DOES IT WORK?

Pennies are made of copper. Copper slowly turns green if it comes into contact with oxygen and a layer of malachite forms. It's just like the bluish-green Statue of Liberty that's made of copper.

The acid in the vinegar makes the reaction between copper and oxygen take place a lot quicker, which means you can see the first traces of green after just one day.

FINGERS!

FLYING FILM ROLL

MAKE AN EXPLODING ROCKET FROM A TUBE!

WHAT DO YOU DO?

Stand the tube upright on a smooth surface.

Pour two fingers of vinegar into it.

Tear off a piece of the paper towel and fold one teaspoon of baking soda in it.

Throw the paper towel envelope into the tube.

Quickly place the top on the tube.

Tip: Start with a bit more baking soda and vinegar if you are using a larger tube to get the best bang.

WHY DOES IT WORK?

This works in the same way as the paint bombs on page 12. The acid from the vinegar and the bicarbonate of the baking soda form a gas (carbon dioxide). So much gas is created that the pressure in the closed tube becomes too much and the top shoots off.

WHAT YOU NEED:

The plastic tube from a roll or film, effervescent tablets, or gum | vinegar | baking soda | paper towels | a teaspoon

KAPOWIE!

FOAMING SNOW

NO SNOW OUTSIDE? MAKE SOME YOURSELF!

> **WHAT YOU NEED:**
> baking soda | a can of foamy shaving cream | glitter (optional)
> vinegar | a bowl | a spoon | a wooden spoon

SUPERSTAR!

WHAT DO YOU DO?

Empty a small box of baking soda into a bowl (you can use less baking soda, but the more the merrier!).

Add a few spoonfuls of glitter to make your snow really glisten.

Spray in some of the shaving cream and mix. Add more shaving cream and mix some more until you have a good snow mixture.

It even feels cold!

OWFOAM!

Try making some snowballs.

Played enough? Pour some vinegar over it and see what happens next.

WHY DOES IT WORK?

As in the other experiments, baking soda combines with the acid in the vinegar to form carbon dioxide. That makes the mixture of shaving cream and baking soda bubble and fizz.

67

RAINBOW ROSES

MAKE ROSES TURN ALL KINDS OF COLORS!

WHAT YOU NEED: ⏱ ⚗⚗⚗
white roses or another white flower | food coloring or tempera paint
water | a sharp knife | narrow glasses | a wooden spoon

FLASHYF

WHAT DO YOU DO?

Get an adult to cut the lower part of the stem of the rose—about four inches—lengthwise into two, three, or four sections. Make sure that the cut sections remain attached to the stem.

Now fill two, three, or four glasses—the same number of sections you have cut the stem of the rose into—with water.

Squirt a few drops of food dye or tempera paint into each glass (a different color in each) and mix well.

Place the glasses close together and place the rose so that a piece of the stem rests in each glass.

Wait for a few hours and see what happens.

Have you ever seen such a fantastic flower?

WHY DOES IT WORK?

A flower drinks water—it sucks the water up through its stem and spreads it through its petals, where it evaporates. If you add a coloring agent to the water, the color remains behind in the petals. The longer the flower stands in the colored water, the brighter the petal color, because more and more coloring remains behind.

BULOUSFLOWERS!!

COLORED CHRISTMAS TREE

CHEER UP YOUR ROOM WITH THIS SPECIAL TREE!

WHAT YOU NEED:
cardboard | food coloring | water
ammonia | bluing | salt | a pair of scissors
a deep plate or shallow dish
a wooden spoon | a tablespoon

WHAT DO YOU DO?

Cut the cardboard into two equal sized triangles about the size of your hand.

Place them with the wide side towards you and a point upwards.

Cut a slit along the middle of one of the triangles from bottom halfway to the top..

Do the same for the other triangle, but start cutting from the peak and cut down to the center. You'll be fitting these two triangles together so that they can stand on their own like a pyramid.

Cut some diagonal zig-zag sections from the slanted sides, so that it looks like a Christmas tree.

Now add the food coloring to the points of all the branches. Use a variety of colors for a festive effect!

In the plate, have an adult help you mix together 3 tablespoons of water with 3 tablespoons of bluing, three tablespoons of salt, and 1½ tablespoons of ammonia. Mix everything together.

Place the two pieces of cardboard tree at right angles, and slide the one with the slit cut in the base onto the one with the slit cut in the point. Stand your tree on the middle of the plate.

Watch it grow a bit each day!

WHY DOES IT WORK?

The cardboard sucks up the liquid mixture. When the liquid reaches the edges of the cardboard, the water evaporates because ammonia speeds up the process. The salt remains behind and forms crystals in the colors that you have painted the branches.

GREATGREENGARDENER!

INVISIBLE INK

WRITE SECRET LETTERS TO YOUR BEST FRIEND!

> **WHAT YOU NEED:**
> lemon | a citrus juicer | a cup | a paint brush
> paper | an iron or hair-dryer

WHAT DO YOU DO?

Press the juice from the lemon and put it in a cup.

Dip your brush in the juice and write or draw a top secret message on the piece of paper.

Leave it to dry.

What do you see? Nothing!

Your friend can read the secret message by heating the piece of paper either with a hair dryer or by ironing the paper (an adult can help but then they can read the message!). You can also place it on a radiator or central heating pipes to make your message visible.

WHY DOES IT WORK?

If you write something with invisible ink, the acid from the lemons seeps into the paper. When you heat the paper, the lemon juice releases a carbon compound that turns brown because it comes into contact with the oxygen in the air. That is what makes your message visible again.

ORANGE LAMP
A GENUINE OLD-FASHIONED OIL LAMP!

WHAT YOU NEED:
an orange | olive oil | matches | a fruit knife

74

WHAT DO YOU DO?

Roll the orange between the palms of your hands, pressing it on all sides. This loosens the skin from the flesh inside.

Now, have an adult cut the orange peel all the way round, just deep enough to reach the flesh.

Wiggle your thumb between the peel and the flesh and loosen the top half of the orange peel all the way round. You'll leave a white point in the middle when you pull it free which will become the wick of your lamp.

Place the half peel with the wick pointing upwards.

Ask the adult to pour olive oil over the wick until the skin is filled halfway up with the oil—the wick should stick out above the oil.

Have an adult hold a burning match against the wick. It may take a while before it catches light, but it will burn for a long time.

With the other part of the orange, you can make a lid for your lamp by easing the peel off the rest of the orange and cutting off the top.

Don't forget to eat the orange!

WHY DOES IT WORK?

The white point in the middle of the orange acts as a wick to suck up the oil. When you light the lamp, only the oil burns. The wick will continue absorbing the oil until there's none left. Only then will the wick burn.

BAKED MARBLES

MAKE YOUR MARBLES INTO WORKS OF ART!

WHAT YOU NEED:

glass marbles | water | an oven | a baking tin | a metal dish or tin

WHAT DO YOU DO?

Have an adult pre-heat the oven to 475°F.

Put the marbles into a baking pan. They must be marbles you can see through. They can be made of colored glass, and can even have swirls in the middle, but opaque marbles won't work.

Get an adult to place the baking pan into the hot oven and wait twenty minutes.

Have a metal dish or pan filled with ice-cold water ready (you can add some ice cubes if you like).

Stand back and get the adult to remove the marbles from the oven and immediately put them into the ice-cold water.

Can you hear them cracking?

Just look how beautiful they are! They are going to be a success at recess!

WHY DOES IT WORK?

When marbles get hot, they expand a bit. If they are then cooled down quickly, the outside cools down first. When the outer layer shrinks, the glass breaks inside the marbles, which can't shrink quickly enough so the marbles stay intact on the outside and crack on the inside.

CRACKCRACKLEPOP!

BOTTLE POPPER
SHOOT A WATER BOTTLE CAP THROUGH THE AIR!

WHAT YOU NEED:
an empty plastic water bottle with a cap

WHAT DO YOU DO?

Tighten the cap on the bottle.

Have an adult start twisting the bottle in the middle. It's difficult at first.

Twist in one direction, until it can't be twisted any more.

Point the opening of the bottle away from you—don't aim at anybody!—and carefully unscrew the cap.

It flies from your fingers!

WHY DOES IT WORK?

The bottle contains air. Because you screwed the cap firmly onto the bottle, the air has nowhere to go.

As you twist the bottle, the pressure in the bottle builds. When you slowly unscrew the cap, it shoots away as the air rushes out.

POP.POP.PLOPPP!

INVISIBLE GLASS

AN AMAZING MAGIC TRICK—MAKE A GLASS DISAPPEAR!

WHAT YOU NEED:
water | vegetable oil or baby oil
a large glass (or wide vase) | a small glass

WHAT DO YOU DO?

Place a small glass in a big glass and fill the small glass with water.

Point out to your audience that the small glass is still clearly visible.

Pour out all the water and tell your audience that you will make the small glass disappear.

Now slowly fill the big glass with oil.

80

FANTASTIC GLASS TRICK!

WHY DOES IT WORK?

You can see something because of the way the light hits it or passes through it. Usually, objects and liquids reflect the light in different ways, so you can easily tell them apart. Oil and glass, however, reflect light in exactly the same way, so you can't see the difference.

THE EGG IN THE BOTTLE

HOW DO YOU GET A BOILED EGG INTO A BOTTLE?

WHAT YOU NEED:

a hard-boiled egg | matches | bottle with a wide neck | paper

SQUEEZE

WHAT DO YOU DO?

Carefully peel the shell off the egg. Check if you can place the egg upside down on the opening of the bottle.

The bottle's neck shouldn't be too narrow or the experiment won't work—an old-fashioned milk bottle is perfect.

Tear a small piece of paper and fold it lengthwise a few times.

Have an adult light the paper.

Throw the paper into the bottle and quickly place the egg on the neck of the bottle.

Will it work?

Once the egg is in the bottle, can you get it out again?

WHY DOES IT WORK?

When air warms up, it expands. This means that the egg is lifted up a little, so that the hot air can escape. After that, there is less air in the bottle than there was at first. When the air cools down, it shrinks and sucks the egg into the bottle. Because the egg is soft and rubbery, it can slip through a hole that is smaller than the egg itself.

You can get the egg out of the bottle again by turning the bottle upside down, so that the egg is as close to the opening as possible, and have an adult blow as hard as possible into the bottle. The air pressure in the bottle is now higher, and that pushes the egg out again.

LOPPLOP!

FIREBALL GRAPE

WHO KNEW GRAPES COULD BE SO EXCITING?

WHAT YOU NEED: grapes | a knife | a plate | a microwave

GREATG

GREAT

APE EXPLOSION!

WHAT DO YOU DO?

On a plate, have an adult help you cut a grape almost in half. Make sure that the two halves are still connected by a thin skin.

Put the plate in the microwave for 15 seconds and watch what happens

Whoever would have thought that one grape could be so spectacular?

WHY DOES IT WORK?

The juice of a grape is full of electrolytes. These electrolytes absorb the energy that a microwave emits. The energy flies back and forth between the two halves of the grape while there is still a little bit of moisture on the piece of skin holding the two halves together. When the connecting skin completely dries out, the energy goes into the air and that becomes a miniature fireball.

EXPLODING MELON

BE CAREFUL—THIS IS A VERY BIG BANG!

MASSIVEMELONMESS!

WHAT YOU NEED: 🎆 🏠🌳 〰 ⛪
a ripe watermelon
rubber bands (about 200, can also be wide)

WHAT DO YOU DO?

This works faster if there are two of you so ask an adult to help.

Stand a watermelon upright.

Put as many rubber bands as possible around the middle of the melon.

Add more and more, over each other.

And even more, and then some more.

You will notice that the melon begins to dent, until it explodes.

WHY DOES IT WORK?

The melon is gradually squeezed by all the elastic bands you put around it. This means that the pressure inside the melon increases. At some point, the outer layer of the melon can't take the pressure and bursts.

BURNING CANDLE WINDMILL

THIS WINDMILL SPINS ALL BY ITSELF!

WHAT DO YOU DO?

Have an adult melt the bottom of the candle with a match until there is a wick at that end as well as one at the top.

Ask an adult to push a nail through the middle of the candle (it works best by heating the nail first in a flame).

Place two wine glasses far enough away from each other so that the candle can easily stand upright between them, with a little room on either side.

Now balance the candle by resting the nail between the two glasses—the ends of the nail should rest on the tops of the glasses. Make sure that the candle is slightly off-center.

Light both ends of the candle and see what happens: the candle begins to sway back and forth.

Will it revolve completely?

WHY DOES IT WORK?

Because the candle is hanging slightly askew, the lower flame first leaks some candle wax, making that part of the candle lighter, so it swings upwards. Then, more candle wax falls from the other end, and that swings upwards and the process repeats.

89

WANDERING WATER

WATCH HOW COLORED WATER CLIMBS AND BLENDS!

COLORFULC

WHAT DO YOU DO?

Fill two glasses with water.

Squirt a few drops of food coloring or tempera paint into each glass (a different color in each.) Mix well. It's best to use primary colors—red, yellow, and/or blue.

Now place a glass with colored water, an empty glass, and then another glass with colored water in a row.

Fold a piece of paper towel lengthwise three times and hang one end into a glass with colored water and fold the other end over the edge of the empty glass.

Do the same with the other glass with colored water, and again hang the other end in the empty glass.

Watch what happens: the water climbs and the two colors meet in the empty glass.

Try all sorts of color combinations.

WHY DOES IT WORK?

Paper towels are made of cellulose fibers. Those fibers contain sugar molecules (but you can't eat the paper!). Water dissolves sugar and searches for a way through the water, past all those sugar molecules. It spreads through the towel from one glass to another.

> **WHAT YOU NEED:** 🧪🧪
> water | food coloring or tempera paint
> at least three glasses | paper towels
> a wooden spoon

MBERS!

GIANT BALLOONS

MAKE GIANT BALLOONS—AGAIN AND AGAIN!

WHAT YOU NEED:

school glue | food coloring or tempera paint
glitter (optional) | borax crystals | a dish
a wooden spoon | wide straws | self-sealing plastic bags

WHAT DO YOU DO?

Squeeze a small bottle of glue into a dish.

Add food coloring or tempera paint and glitter until you are really happy with it!

Have an adult slowly stir in borax. Borax is poisonous, so wash your hands before you touch any food.

Your mixture is ready when it is still squishy but you can pull bits of it away from the rest.

Take a dollop of the mixture, push it into the end of a straw and blow. (Make sure the mixture doesn't touch the end of the straw you're blowing into.)

You may need to practice, but in no time you'll be producing amazing bubbles!

You can keep the balloon mixture in a plastic bag, so that you can use it as often as you like.

WHY DOES IT WORK?

The glue contains small particles of plastic. Borax is a mineral salt that joins the small plastic particles together in such a way that it forms a squishy plastic mass. In fact, you're blowing plastic balloons!

BIGBIGGERBIGGESTBALLOONS!

THE BALLOON OVER THE CANDLE

A BALLOON THAT CAN WITHSTAND A FLAME? IS THAT POSSIBLE?

WHAT DO YOU DO?

Have an adult light the candle. Blow up a balloon and hold it just above the candle.

What happens?

Now use a funnel to pour some water into a balloon. Blow it up.

What happens when an adult holds the balloon over the candle? Can it handle the heat?

WHY DOES IT WORK?

If you hold a balloon that contains only air above a candle flame, the plastic of the balloon melts. As the layer that holds the balloon together gets thinner, the pressure of the air in the balloon makes it burst.

If there is water in the balloon, the water absorbs the heat from the candle flame. That's why the balloon doesn't melt. With no weak spot, the balloon won't burst.

WHAT YOU NEED:
a candle | matches | balloons | water | a funnel

KINETIC SAND

MAKE SUPER SAND YOURSELF!

WHAT DO YOU DO?

In a dish, mix together two cups of sand, a cup of corn starch and half a cup of baby oil. Your sand is ready!

After you've finished playing with it, store the sand in a jar or plastic bag so that it doesn't dry out.

WHY DOES IT WORK?

The corn starch combines with the sand and the baby oil to make one mass. Corn starch contains starch that works like an elastic binding agent. That's why kinetic sand is much more pliable that ordinary sand. The baby oil also prevents the sand from drying out too quickly.

MICROWAVE CLAY

YOU'RE NEVER TOO OLD TO PLAY WITH CLAY!

WHAT DO YOU DO?

In the microwave-safe bowl, mix together 2 cups of flour, 2 cups of water, 1 cup of salt, 1 tablespoon of oil, 1 tablespoon of food coloring and 1 teaspoon of cream of tartar.

Mix thoroughly.

Have an adult place the uncovered mixture in the microwave and heat it for three minutes on the highest setting.

Have an adult stir the mixture thoroughly and put it back. Now heat it for another two minutes on the highest setting.

Let the clay cool, then knead it well.

Keep the clay in a jar or container that has a lid when you're not playing with it, so that it doesn't dry out.

WHY DOES IT WORK?

Flour contains proteins. In the heat of the microwave, these proteins combine with the water to form a squishy elastic mass. The cream of tartar increases the elasticity. The oil helps the clay stay moist without getting too sticky. The salt is a preservative and makes the clay last longer and prevents it from turning moldy.

WHAT YOU NEED:
corn starch | water | food coloring or tempera paint
ice cube trays | a bowl | a cup

WHY DOES IT WORK?

The corn starch, the water and the coloring agent form a liquid paint which you can also use as liquid sidewalk paint.

When it freezes, the paint becomes hard enough to use as chalk.

You'll notice that it melts in the heat and the color once again becomes liquid on the sidewalk.

100